# IRON WILL

# SURVIVING IN SPACE

Kristin J. Russo

full tilt PRESS

# Surviving in Space
Iron Will

Full Tilt Press
42982 Osgood Road
Fremont, CA 94539
readfulltilt.com

Full Tilt Press publications may be purchased for educational, business, or sales promotional use.

**Editorial Credits**

Design and layout by Sara Radka
Edited by Lauren Dupuis-Perez
Copyedited by Renae Gilles

**Image Credits**

Getty Images: Central Press, 11 (top), Central Press, 44 (top), E+, 36 (middle), 37 (top), Evening Standard, 19, Hulton Archive, 13, iStockphoto, 45, Keystone/Hulton Archive, 7, MPI/Neil Armstrong, 3 (top), 15, NASA, 25, NASA/Newsmakers, 3 (bottom), 17 (top), Space Frontiers, 10; NASA: JSC, 37 (middle), 9; Pixabay: lumina_obscura, background, Pexels, 11 (Moon), Wikilmages, 11 (Earth); Shutterstock: Bogdan Syrotynskyi, 38–39, Castelski, 2–3 (background), Mrkevvzime, 36 (top), NikoNomad, cover, Rick Partington, 36 (bottom), Vadim Sadovski, 4; Wikimedia: Alexander Mokletsov, 22, de:Benutzer:HPH, 21, German Federal Archives, 23, NASA, 3 (middle), 17 (bottom), 27, 28, 33, 35, 37 (bottom), 43, 44 (bottom), NASA/Crew of STS-132, 34, NASA/Crew of STS-86, 29, NASA/James Blair, 31, Wknight94, 16

ISBN: 978-1-62920-806-0 (library binding)
ISBN: 978-1-62920-814-5 (ePub)

full tilt PRESS

# CONTENTS

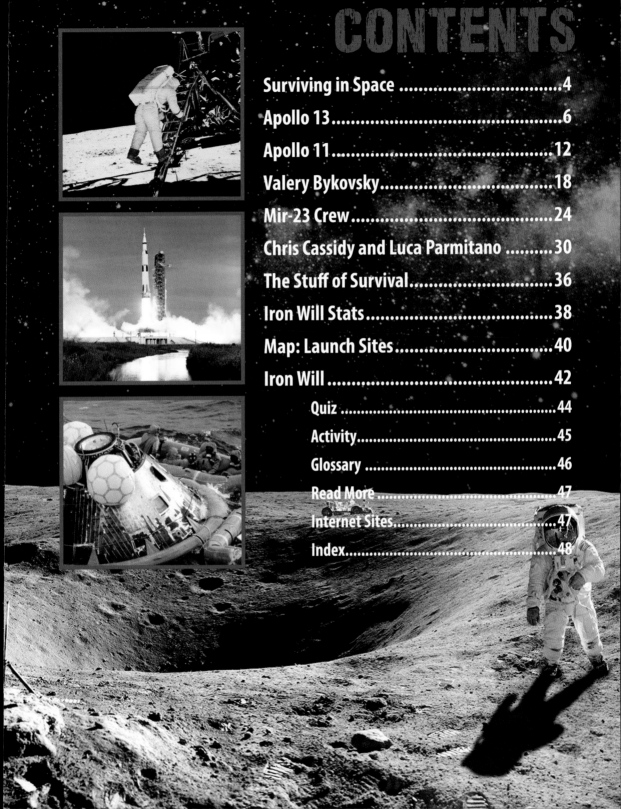

# SURVIVING IN SPACE

Humankind has wondered about outer space for thousands of years. People once thought the moon was a god. Space explorers have discovered the truth about many things that were once mysteries. Astronauts continue to push the boundaries of space exploration. They want to find out more.

As astronauts spin through orbit, they can watch the sun rise up to 16 times per day. Viewing Earth from thousands of miles away is a magical experience. But traveling to outer space is one of the most dangerous journeys a person can take. Astronauts prepare for every type of emergency. Unfortunately, they can't plan for the unexpected. When things go wrong, astronauts go without power or even air to breathe! Only astronauts with an **iron will** can survive when disaster strikes in space.

**iron will:** having a strong feeling that you are going to do something and that you will not allow anything to stop you

# APOLLO 13

## United States

1969

Before John L. Swigert became an astronaut, he had been a US Air Force pilot.

Jack Swigert had never flown in space before. He had worked behind the scenes on NASA missions. He had never left Earth's **atmosphere**. Swigert looked forward to landing on the moon. But Apollo 13 commander Jim Lovell was not happy when Swigert was assigned to the crew at the last minute. Another astronaut had been exposed to German measles and was not allowed to fly. Swigert took his place.

In April 1970, the crew had been in space for two days. They had almost reached the moon when the unthinkable happened. An **oxygen** tank exploded. The crew was stuck in space with little heat, food, or water. The mission would never land on the moon. Instead, the crew would be lucky just to survive.

"Houston, we've had a problem here."

**JACK SWIGERT**

**atmosphere:** a layer of gases surrounding Earth

**oxygen:** a colorless gas that people need to breathe in order to survive

# A PROBLEM

Apollo 13's spacecraft was made of two different spaceships. They were joined by a tunnel. The two spaceships were named *Odyssey* and *Aquarius*. The team flew into space in *Odyssey*. They planned to use *Aquarius* to land on the moon.

The astronauts had been in space about 56 hours. Suddenly, a controller at NASA headquarters in Houston, Texas, saw a flashing light. It was a warning about low pressure in a hydrogen tank on *Odyssey*. Back on *Odyssey*, Swigert went to investigate. He thought the hydrogen tank needed a "cryo stir." This meant flipping a switch that would mix the hydrogen and keep it safe for use.

But when the switch was flipped, disaster struck. Exposed wires from a nearby oxygen tank sparked a fire. One oxygen tank was destroyed, and another was damaged. Without oxygen, the crew would not be able to breathe. Swigert quickly reported to Mission Control. "Houston, we've had a problem here."

The crew moved quickly to *Aquarius*. But *Aquarius* had no heat shield. This meant it would burn up when it entered Earth's atmosphere on the way back. The crew could breathe inside *Aquarius*, but they wouldn't survive reentry. They wouldn't reach **splashdown**.

---

**splashdown:** the splash-landing of a manned spacecraft into the ocean

Apollo 13 astronauts could see the damage to the spacecraft. They took photos of it near the end of their mission.

# NO HEAT, LITTLE FOOD

Before the explosion, the crew had set the spacecraft's course. They were aiming for the moon. But they had to change course to get home. The crew worked with Mission Control. They came up with a plan. Five hours after the explosion, they burned fuel. This moved the spacecraft in the right direction. As they approached the moon, they did it again to stop the landing. The plan worked. Apollo 13 was headed in the right direction.

Apollo 13 crew after rescue

The astronauts huddled in *Aquarius*. They had no heat and suffered in the cold. Some of their food was ruined. They had to conserve water. But they had enough air to breathe. At Mission Control in Houston, controllers worked hard. They did all they could to keep *Aquarius* operating. They had to support the lives of the astronauts on board. The astronauts moved from *Aquarius* back into the damaged *Odyssey* as they neared Earth's atmosphere.

Finally on April 17, 1970, the Apollo 13 *Odyssey* command **module** made a safe splashdown in the Pacific Ocean. The crew was picked up by helicopter and brought to the USS *Iwo Jima*. The Navy ship had been waiting for splashdown only 4 miles (6.4 kilometers) away.

**module:** a small section of a spacecraft

**protocol:** an official set of rules; a way of doing something

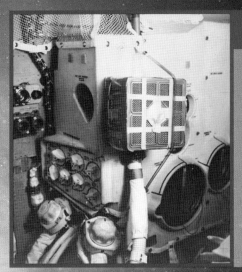

## LEARNING FROM PAST MISTAKES

After the Apollo 13 disaster, NASA made changes to space mission **protocol**. Future space missions included extra oxygen to breathe and water to drink. This extra oxygen and water would not be needed to keep the ship operating. Changes also included more battery power and a different kind of heating tube for cryo tanks to keep them from exploding during a cryo stir.

# APOLLO 13 FLIGHT PATH

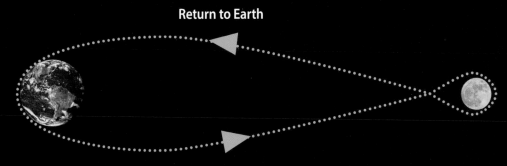

Return to Earth

Path to the Moon

# APOLLO 11

## United States

### 1969

Apollo 11 was launched into space on a rocket.

"We would either land on the moon, we would crash attempting to land, or we would abort."

**GENE KRANZ**

It was July 16, 1969. NASA's Apollo 11 mission launched from the Kennedy Space Center in Cape Canaveral, Florida. Astronauts Neil Armstrong, Michael Collins, and Edwin "Buzz" Aldrin were on board. They were going to be the first humans on the moon. Four days later, Apollo 11 was about 33,000 feet (10,000 meters) from the moon's surface. Aldrin and Armstrong began their descent toward the moon in the **lunar** module. But then, Armstrong made a frightening discovery.

Armstrong called Mission Control in Houston, Texas. "Program alarm," he said. Something was terribly wrong. It looked like the computer system was in trouble. This was vital equipment that the astronauts needed to complete the landing. It would take an iron will to find and solve the problem before it was too late.

**lunar:** having to do with the moon

# ERROR CODE 1202

"Error code 1202" popped up on the screens at Mission Control in Houston. No one knew exactly what it meant. Controllers rushed to find the source of the problem. It looked like the landing module was low on fuel.

"Give us a reading on that program alarm," Armstrong demanded. Mission Control could hear the tension in his voice. They told Armstrong that there was nothing to worry about. They had enough fuel on the landing module. The plan to land on the moon was on.

Gene Kranz, flight director for the lunar landing, said later, "We would either land on the moon, we would crash attempting to land, or we would abort. The two final outcomes were not good."

Communication grew spotty as Armstrong steered toward the moon. He guided the module around a field of boulders to a safe landing site. He did this without help from Mission Control.

When Buzz Aldrin stepped off the lunar module onto the ground, he was only the second person to ever walk on the moon.

# SUCCESS

Armstrong's lunar landing was a success. The first people had finally landed on the moon. Armstrong and Aldrin gathered data on the moon's surface. Then they flew the lunar module back to the command module. There, Collins was waiting for them.

The lunar module attached to the command module. Armstrong and Aldrin climbed inside with Collins. The lunar module was left behind. It crashed back down to the moon. The Apollo 11 crew made a safe splashdown in the Pacific Ocean on July 24, 1969. The astronauts were picked up by the USS *Hornet*.

## MOON ROCKS

Neil Armstrong and Buzz Aldrin returned from their trip to the moon with samples of rock and soil from the moon's surface. They collected a type of rock called basalt. Basalt is made by magma from volcanoes. The astronauts found basalt rocks that are about 3.7 billion years old. Scientists believe that volcanoes flowed on the moon at about the same time dinosaurs roamed Earth.

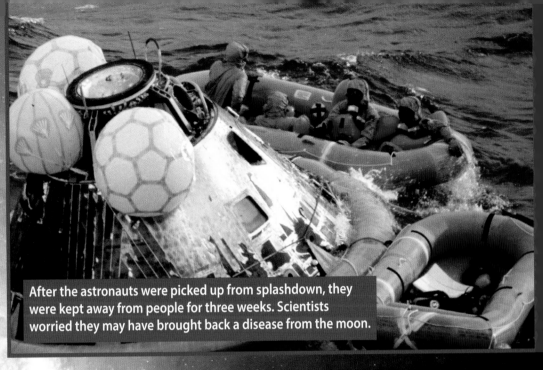

After the astronauts were picked up from splashdown, they were kept away from people for three weeks. Scientists worried they may have brought back a disease from the moon.

## APOLLO 11 LANDING SITE

100 km

# VALERY BYKOVSKY

Russia

1963

Valery Bykovsky earned the Soviet Union's highest honor, the Order of the Red Star.

"There was a powerful explosion when the cabin **hatch** blew off, and I was ejected from the capsule in my seat two seconds later."

**VALERY BYKOVSKY**

Valery Bykovsky had always wanted to fly. He took flying lessons when he was 16 years old. At age 25, he became a fighter pilot for the Union of Soviet Socialist Republics (USSR). The USSR was a country in Eastern Europe that is now called Russia. Bykovsky wanted to explore outer space. Soon he began training to become a cosmonaut, the Russian word for astronaut.

Bykovsky wanted to do something that no other person had ever done. On June 14, 1963, he undertook his biggest challenge—to fly the longest solo mission in outer space. Bykovsky set out to orbit Earth 81 times. No one had ever been in space for that long. Would he get hurt? Would he survive? Bykovsky was about to find out.

**hatch:** a door to the outside of an aircraft

# THE LAUNCH

Bykovsky's launch in the Vostok 5 spaceship was set for June 7, 1963. That day, there were high winds. This made it too dangerous for the craft to take off. Then a technical problem postponed the launch again. A third problem, a **solar flare** storm, caused another delay. Bykovsky's spaceship could not take off until June 14.

Finally, conditions were perfect. Sometimes after liftoff, astronauts feel as if they will pass out. This is due to "**g-loading**." G-loading happens when astronauts fly through Earth's atmosphere very fast.

Gravity was no longer a problem when Bykovsky reached outer space. Bykovsky floated freely in space without the force of gravity weighing him down. But there were other problems. There was an unexpected shift in pressure in the atmosphere. One of the engines wasn't working very well. These issues sent the spacecraft off course. As a result, no one knew exactly where Bykovsky's ship would land when—or if—he completed his mission.

**solar flare:** a sudden flash of brightness caused by an explosion on the sun

**g-loading:** the effect of gravity on a pilot while he or she is flying in Earth's atmosphere

The Vostok was the first spacecraft to carry humans into space.

# FEARLESS FLYER

Bykovsky didn't let these problems scare him. He had an iron will. He enjoyed floating around in the gravity-free cabin. Bykovsky described his view of Earth from outer space. "I could make out islands easily and recognized Leningrad, the Nile, and Cairo. At sea, I could see the wakes of ships and large barges."

Bykovsky's spaceship reentered Earth's atmosphere on June 19. His landing was violent. "There was a powerful explosion when the cabin hatch blew off," he said. "I was ejected from the capsule in my seat two seconds later. I landed between two trees in a **steppe**-like region." Local villagers drove Bykovsky back to the spacecraft. It had landed about 1 mile (1.6 km) away. He radioed Mission Control to tell them where he landed. He stayed the night in the village of Kustan. The next day, he was picked up by Soviet officials.

## FIRST WOMAN IN SPACE

While Bykovsky was setting the record for the longest solo space flight, Valentina Tereshkova became the first woman in space. The Soviet cosmonaut launched Vostok 6 on June 16, 1963. She orbited Earth 48 times in 3 days before making a parachute landing near the Kazakhstan-Mongolia-China border. Tereshkova got in trouble for having dinner with local villagers before undergoing a medical examination after she landed. It was her only space flight.

---

**steppe:** a large area of flat, unforested grassland

Bykovsky and fellow cosmonaut Sigmund Jahn worked together in space after Bykovsky's solo mission. They did many experiments in space.

# VOSTOK 5 LAUNCH AND LANDING SITES

**WHERE VOSTOK 5 LAUNCHED**
Baikonur Cosmodrome

**WHERE BYKOVSKY LANDED**
Near Karatal, Kazakhstan

LANDING SITE ☆

BAIKONUR ☆
COSMODROME

☆ Starting Location

★ Ending Location

# MIR-23 CREW

Mir Space Station

1997

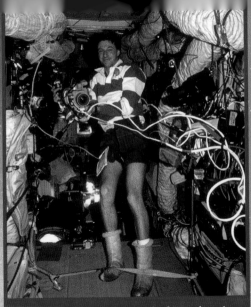

Michael Foale spent a total of 374 days in space on multiple trips.

"There are no heroes if nothing's going wrong. There are only heroes when things go wrong."

**MICHAEL FOALE**

Mir was a Russian **space station**. Astronauts from many different countries traveled there. They lived there while working in space. Supply ships brought supplies to the astronauts on board. Astronauts planned and practiced all the tasks they did in space. This included **docking** a supply ship.

In 1997, Russian cosmonauts Vasily Tsibliev and Aleksandr Lazutkin and NASA astronaut Michael Foale were on board Mir. Their task was to dock a nearby cargo ship called *Progress*. They used remote controls to drive *Progress* toward a module on Mir called *Spektr*. The team could only guess how close *Progress* was and how fast it was going by watching it on a computer screen and through a small window. This wasn't enough.

*Progress* moved too fast. Tsibliev couldn't get the aircraft to slow down. *Progress* sped toward *Spektr*.

**space station:** a spacecraft where people live in order to do research and experiments in space

**docking:** attaching one spacecraft or module to another

# THE CRASH

*Progress* crashed into *Spektr* and ripped a hole in the module's **hull**. The disaster knocked out power and sent oxygen spilling into outer space. The crew on board scrambled to save their oxygen by pulling out wires so they could find the hole in the walls of the module. This caused power outages in other areas of the ship. It seemed as if the crew on board was doomed.

The collision also caused Mir to spin out of control. The crew couldn't use tools that would slow down the spin because they didn't have power. The Moscow control center back on Earth could help, but they didn't know how fast Mir was spinning. They didn't have the information they needed to do anything.

First, the crew on Mir plugged the oxygen leaks. Then, they had to figure out how fast they were spinning. Foale looked out a window. He used his thumb to measure Mir's position against the stars. He did some math and sent the information to Mission Control. Foale's math worked, and the space station stopped spinning. But their troubles weren't over yet.

---

**hull:** the main section of a ship or aircraft

The Mir space station was planned to orbit Earth for 5 years. Instead, it lasted in orbit for 15 years!

# REPAIR IT FAST

Mir had no electricity and no heat. This caused moisture to cover the wires and computer equipment. Foale tried to save what he could. "Fifty percent of my time was spent just mopping up water. It was like cave diving, going into a dark module with a full-length suit on," Foale said. He used old clothes to mop up the water. He also had a device that sucked water into an airtight bag.

Wires had also been pulled out after the collision. The crew worked for weeks to reattach them. More than a month later, a supply ship arrived. It brought equipment the crew needed to fix the rest of the ship. With a shared iron will, the crew on Mir had survived the terrible collision in space.

## THE LIFE OF MIR

Russia launched the first piece of Mir into orbit on February 20, 1986. The first cosmonaut crew arrived in March. It orbited Earth more than 86,000 times. On March 23, 2001, Mir reentered Earth's atmosphere. It broke into pieces. Pieces that didn't burn up landed in the southern Pacific Ocean. People from Japan to New Zealand reported seeing fire and light as Mir fell from the sky.

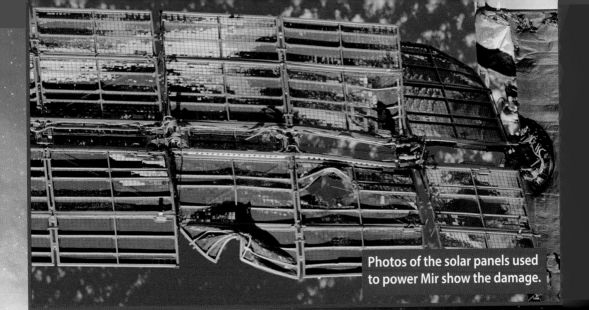

Photos of the solar panels used to power Mir show the damage.

# VISITORS TO MIR

These countries all sent astronauts to the Mir space station.

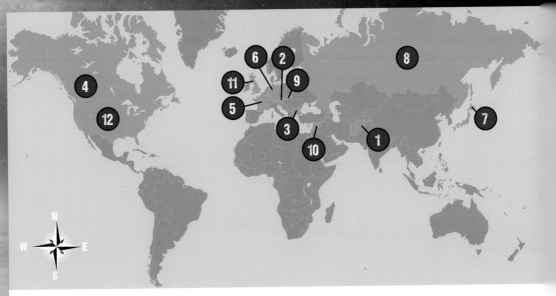

1. Afghanistan
2. Austria
3. Bulgaria
4. Canada
5. France
6. Germany
7. Japan
8. Russia
9. Slovakia
10. Syria
11. United Kingdom
12. United States

# CHRIS CASSIDY

## AND

# LUCA PARMITANO

## International Space Station
## 2013

Luca Parmitano is part of the European Astronaut Corps for the European Space Agency.

"I can't even be sure that the next time I breathe I will fill my lungs with air and not liquid."

**LUCA PARMITANO**

On July 16, 2013, two astronauts were living and working aboard the International Space Station (ISS). They were NASA astronaut Chris Cassidy and European astronaut Luca Parmitano. Their task for the day was to go on a space walk outside the station. They needed to make routine repairs.

A space walk is also called an extravehicular activity (EVA). Parmitano loved going on EVAs. He enjoyed spending time outside in the strange, quiet world of outer space. But he knew that EVAs can be very dangerous. "Let me tell you, the environment we work in is incredibly harsh. It will kill you if you make mistakes," said Parmitano.

Parmitano followed all of the safety rules before leaving the space station. But something happened that no one expected.

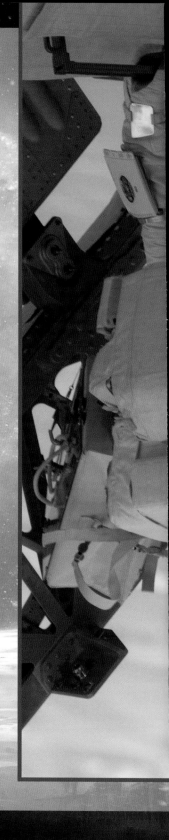

# WATER IN SPACE

While working outside, Parmitano felt water on his neck. He told Mission Control. They thought it was a small leak from a drinking-water bag. Then a drop landed on Parmitano's tongue. It tasted metallic. It wasn't drinking water. Something far more serious was happening. A cooling pump in Parmitano's space suit had failed. Water was leaking from the pump into his helmet.

The astronauts stopped working. They headed back inside. An antenna blocked Parmitano's path. He had to flip around to get past it. The water in his helmet rushed to the top of his head and covered his nose and eyes. He couldn't see and could barely breathe.

"By now, the upper part of the helmet is full of water, and I can't even be sure that the next time I breathe I will fill my lungs with air and not liquid," Parmitano later wrote.

Parmitano tried to remain calm. He used his safety **tether** to guide him back to the hatch. A crewmate opened the door. Parmitano rushed inside with Cassidy right behind him. But he wasn't safe yet.

---

**tether:** a rope or chain used to tie or connect something to make it safe and secure

During an EVA, astronauts are attached to the space station by a tether most of the time. This prevents them from floating away into space.

The module inside the space station had to fill with air before he could remove his helmet. Without oxygen in the capsule, neither Parmitano nor Cassidy would be able to breathe. They had to wait for the air pressure to rise. It was a long and painful wait. The water covered Parmitano's nose. Since he was still flipped around, he had a small area clear of water near his mouth. Cassidy wasn't sure if it was enough. He feared his friend was drowning.

After several minutes, finally it was time. The other astronauts on board opened the module and rushed to Parmitano's aid. They pulled off his helmet. Parmitano could breathe! "Thanks, guys," he told his friends. He was finally safe!

After Parmitano's near-disaster, scientists redesigned NASA space suits. Now there is an extra breathing tube for astronauts to use if a helmet ever fills with water again.

## THE INTERNATIONAL SPACE STATION

Construction began on the International Space Station in 1998. People have been living and working at the station since 2000. The last piece of construction went up in 2011. At that point, the station was complete. Six people can live on board at once. It has five bedrooms, two bathrooms, and a gymnasium, as well as science labs from the United States, Russia, Japan, and several countries in Europe.

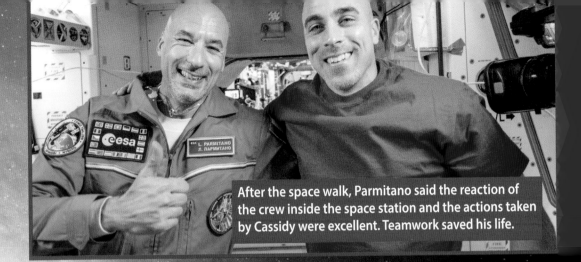

After the space walk, Parmitano said the reaction of the crew inside the space station and the actions taken by Cassidy were excellent. Teamwork saved his life.

# ISS ORBIT PATH

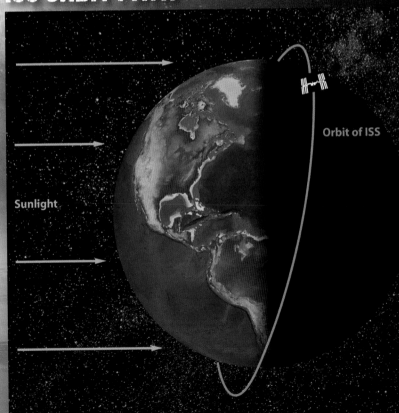

Orbit of ISS

Sunlight

Surviving in space is not easy. Even simple supplies can help people solve major problems.. These are some of the resources that can help save lives.

## OXYGEN

There is no oxygen for people to breathe in outer space. Astronauts must bring their own supply of air to breathe. Oxygen supplies can come from a spaceship or attached to a space suit.

## FOOD AND WATER

No food grows on the moon or on any of the planets scientists have discovered so far. Astronauts must bring their own food and water with them when they travel into space.

## SPACE SUIT

Humans can live for only 15 seconds without the protection of a space suit in outer space. People need a special suit to protect them.

## EXERCISE

Astronauts need to keep their muscles strong in an environment that has no gravity. On the International Space Station, they use exercise machines for at least two hours per day to keep their muscles from becoming too weak.

## TRAINING

Astronauts need years of training to prepare to travel in space. They train underwater to get used to living in the weightlessness of space.

## COMMUNICATION

Astronauts must be able to communicate with Mission Control. Scientists on Earth play an important role in helping astronauts complete missions successfully.

# IRON WILL STATS

Scientists guess that there are almost **130 million** pieces of space junk floating around in outer space. **Space junk** can be anything from rocket fragments to satellites to pieces of equipment dropped while building the International Space Station.

Soviet cosmonaut **Yuri Gagarin** became the first human in space. He completed a 108-minute flight into orbit on April 12, 1961.

The crew of NASA's Apollo 10 mission holds the record for the **fastest human travel**. They reached a top speed of 24,791 miles (39,897 km) per hour when they returned to Earth on May 26, 1969.

Astronauts **Franklin Chang-Díaz** and **Jerry Ross** share the record for most space flights, with a total of seven each. Chang-Díaz traveled to space seven times between 1986 and 2002. Ross traveled to space seven times between 1985 and 2002.

The cosmonaut who first completed a space walk almost didn't make it home safely. **Alexei Leonov** had trouble returning to his spacecraft when his space suit ballooned after a 12-minute space walk on March 18, 1965.

The youngest person in space, Soviet cosmonaut **Gherman Titov**, was 25 when he launched into orbit in August 1961. His mission lasted 25 hours. During this time, he became the first person to fall asleep in outer space.

Russian cosmonaut **Valery Polyakov** holds the record for the longest time spent in space during one trip. Polyakov lived on board the Mir space station for **438 days**, from January 1994 to March 1995.

The first American astronaut in space, Alan Shepard, holds the record for the **shortest space mission**. On May 5, 1961, Shepard's space flight lasted just 15 minutes. He splashed down in the Atlantic Ocean just 302 miles (486 km) away from where he launched.

# LAUNCH SITES

Space can be very dangerous. Getting to space is also a big risk. There are spaceports all over the world that are built as launching sites to send people and supplies into orbit.

## 1. CAPE CANAVERAL

*Cape Canaveral, Florida*

Cape Canaveral is located in Florida, off of Canaveral Island. It is the main launching site for NASA. Launching rockets is dangerous work. More than 30 people have died at Cape Canaveral while building or maintaining the launch site.

## 2. BAIKONUR COSMODROME

*Kazakhstan*

This Russian launch site is located in Kazakhstan. The climate can be very harsh. Temperatures can drop to –40° Fahrenheit (–40° Celsius). It has been in operation since 1957.

### 3. XICHANG SATELLITE LAUNCH CENTER

*Xichang City, China*

This is China's busiest launch site. It opened in 1984. Located just outside of Xichang City, the Space Launch Center is most often used for launching satellites, but has also launched missiles into space.

### 4. GUIANA SPACE CENTER

*French Guiana*

Located in Kourou in French Guiana, the Space Center is the main launch site for France and other European countries. It is known for launching large Automated Transfer Vehicles that bring supplies to the International Space Station.

# IRON WILL

Curiosity drove the first astronauts into outer space. They looked up into the great unknown and decided they wanted answers. What is out there? What does space look like? What does it feel like? They conquered their fears and flew beyond Earth's atmosphere to explore.

But their space quests weren't easy. Space is a harsh environment. There is no oxygen to breathe. There is no gravity to keep people and items in place. Scientists who choose to explore space must be ready for disaster to strike at any time. They must be brave enough to face unexpected emergencies and to solve unimaginable problems.

The more astronauts explore space, the more they realize there is much that we don't understand. We need their imagination and skill to find answers. Space explorers also need courage and an iron will. Because outer space is risky—even fatal—to those who don't respect its dangers.

The Saturn V Rocket sent astronauts into space for the Apollo program. It sent men to the moon!

# QUIZ

**1** What colorless gas do all humans need to breathe in order to survive?

**2** What was the name of the spaceship where Apollo 13's crew took refuge in when *Odyssey* was damaged?

**3** What type of rock did the Apollo 11 crew bring back from the moon?

**4** What is another term for a space walk?

**5** What is the name of the Russian space station that orbited Earth 86,000 times from 1986 to 2001?

**6** How did NASA redesign space suits after Luca Parmitano's near-disaster?

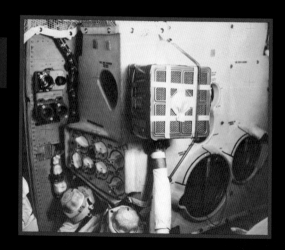

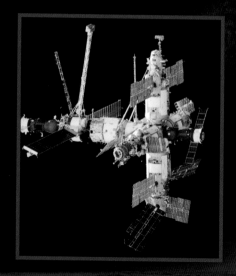

# ACTIVITY

What does it take to become an astronaut? Go to your library to check out books about space. Ask your librarian and your teacher to help you find websites that will tell you what you need to do to become an astronaut. Answer these questions with the research you have done.

1   What subjects do you need to study in school?

2   What places train astronauts?

3   What government agencies choose astronauts and send them on space missions?

Finally, write a three-paragraph plan for becoming an astronaut. Decide if becoming an astronaut is something you would like to do. Share your plan with your friends and classmates.

# GLOSSARY

**atmosphere:** a layer of gases surrounding Earth

**docking:** attaching one spacecraft or module to another

**g-loading:** the effect of gravity on a pilot while he or she is flying in Earth's atmosphere

**hatch:** a door to the outside of an aircraft

**hull:** the main section of a ship or aircraft

**iron will:** having a strong feeling that you are going to do something and that you will not allow anything to stop you

**lunar:** having to do with the moon

**module:** a small section of a spacecraft

**oxygen:** a colorless gas that people need to breathe in order to survive

**protocol:** an official set of rules; a way of doing something

**space station:** a spacecraft where people live in order to do research and experiments in space

**splashdown:** the splash-landing of a manned spacecraft into the ocean

**solar flare:** a sudden flash of brightness caused by an explosion on the sun

**steppe:** a large area of flat, unforested grassland

**tether:** a rope or chain used to tie or connect something to make it safe and secure

# READ MORE

Hutchinson, Patricia. *Exploring beyond Our Solar System.* Wonders of Space. North Mankato, Minn.: The Child's World, Inc., 2016.

Hutchinson, Patricia. *The First Moon Landing.* Wonders of Space. North Mankato, Minn.: The Child's World, Inc., 2016.

Labrecque, Ellen. *Yvonne Brill and Satellite Propulsion.* Women Innovators. Ann Arbor, Mich.: Cherry Lake Publishing, 2017.

Ringstad, Arnold. *Space Missions of the 21st Century.* Wonders of Space. North Mankato, Minn.: The Child's World, Inc., 2016.

Russo, Kristin J. *Space Facts or Fibs?* North Mankato, Minn.: Capstone Press, 2018.

# INTERNET SITES

https://www.space.com/11337-human-spaceflight-records-50th-anniversary.html
**Learn about recordbreaking astronauts and space missions.**

https://www.nasa.gov/kidsclub/index.html
**Play puzzles and games while learning about outer space.**

https://www.natgeokids.com/uk/discover/science/space/ten-facts-about-space
**Read surprising facts about outer space.**

https://www.nasa.gov/audience/forstudents/k-4/stories/nasa-knows/what-is-the-iss-k4.html
**Read about the International Space Station.**

# INDEX